D1032895

MULES & MEMORIES

A PHOTO DOCUMENTARY
OF THE TOBACCO FARMER

J.C. Perry, Georgia

"Before I got old enough to raise tobacco on my own, I helped other people raise it. After that I sharecropped for two or three years. Then I rented. I bought this farm in 1936.

"Back then I was young and afraid of a debt. So I didn't grow any more tobacco than I could work myself. I still use the old ways mostly, though I'm growing more tobacco than before.

"There ain't no cheap way to farm anymore. A one-horse farm just cain't take care of you. If you ain't able to expand and have a big operation, you just cain't make it. But I've got the country in my blood. I don't want to move in close to people. I love to go to town; but I want to go to the country to go home.

"I couldn't have made a living without my tobacco. Oh, I might have existed; but I wouldn't have fixed my house up, or sent six of my ten children to college. I want to credit tobacco with that, and I'm telling the truth when I say it.

"Believe it or not, when I was growing up, if a child was wormy, our doctor put him on chewing tobacco! I don't know whether it helped or not, but that skinny, wobbly-kneed kid would go to fattening up. And now he's most likely a healthy, grown man, and still chewing!

"I ain't never knowed that much about pleasure, not even yet. But having to work hard, now, I know about that."

MULES & MEMORIES

A PHOTO DOCUMENTARY OF THE TOBACCO FARMER

PHOTOGRAPHS AND INTERVIEWS BY
PAMELA BAREFOOT

CHAPTER INTRODUCTIONS BY BURT KORNEGAY

Distributed by John F. Blair, Publisher,
Winston-Salem, North Carolina

Dedicated to the American tobacco farmer

Jacket and Book Design by Bruce W. Smith
Printed by W.M. Brown & Son, Richmond, Virginia
Distributed by John F. Blair, Publisher
                    1406 Plaza Drive
                    Winston-Salem, North Carolina 27103
Copyright © 1978 by Barefoot Productions
First Edition Library of Congress Catalogue Card Number 78-72529
ISBN 0-9602024-0-4

CONTENTS

ACKNOWLEDGMENTS

Thanks and appreciation to the National Endowment for the Humanities for a grant which made possible much of the research for this book; to Universal Leaf Tobacco Company and Kemp Dozier for their continual faith and support at times when it was needed most; to Governor Jim Hunt of North Carolina for his thoughtful letter; to the Tobacco Institute, the Tobacco Tax Council, the Tobacco Growers' Information Committee, the Virginia Farm Bureau, and Carrington and Michaux for their encouragement and assistance; to American Brands for permission to reprint the advertisement from the 1939 issue of LIFE magazine; to John Torres, Jr. for encouraging me to "think big"; to Medford Taylor for his photographic editing and guidance; to my cousin, Burt, for help in editing interviews and compiling the text; to Tim Oksman, my attorney, for keeping things from falling apart; to Betty Dillon for a little bit of everything; to Jim Green for keeping a lit candle in the window; to everyone who helped in any way to make this dream come true; and to the wonderful people throughout Tobaccoland who shared their hearts and time with me, and now, through this book, are sharing them with the world. Many thanks to all of you.

STATE OF NORTH CAROLINA
OFFICE OF THE GOVERNOR
RALEIGH 27611

JAMES B. HUNT, JR.
GOVERNOR

Dear Pamela:

I want to congratulate you on your excellent book "Mules and Memories."

I grew up on a tobacco farm, and I've been involved in tobacco farming all my life. I started out handing, then I trucked, and finally became "a man" and began cropping. I have never seen or heard a more sensitive and accurate portrayal of what the tobacco farmer's life is like than yours.

Almost anybody can write a book, but few people can capture in words and photographs the human side of tobacco farming—the heat, the back-breaking work, the economic uncertainties and the fundamental love and respect for the land and the crop.

You have done that, and, because of your work, I hope that millions of Americans will have a better understanding of the people who grow tobacco.

My warmest personal regards.

Sincerely,

Jim Hunt

TO THE READER

One July morning several years back, an uncle roused us at dawn to help with the first tobacco barning of the season. Our aunt showed up at the barn bringing along our two-year-old cousin, Kevin. Throughout the morning, between moments of astonishment whenever a tractor chugged up with a trailer-load of freshly cropped leaves, little Kevin "helped" the adults pass the sticks of tied tobacco into the barn to be hung and cured. He was doing his share in a two-year-old way. Later that day word came that Grandpa, our oldest living relative, had died. The family left immediately for his house. A few workers remained just long enough to get the last sticks of tobacco tied and hung in the barn.

A week after the funeral some of us drove to the family's private graveyard to collect the many wreaths which had been placed on the grave. We carried them in the back of a pick-up truck to the tobacco packhouse on Grandpa's farm where we had decided to leave them temporarily. Lining up, we began to hand the wreaths, one by one, from the truck into the packhouse—just the way we had passed in the first sticks of cured tobacco the day before.

We thought about little Kevin play-passing tobacco sticks earlier in the week, and about this line of kinfolk silently handing wreaths. From the cradle to the grave, how pervasively the methods and customs of tobacco farming had shaped our lives—had really given us a way of life, a way of expressing life, whether in happiness or grief! Talking about it later, we realized that tobacco farming possessed a rhythm and dignity of its own, a beauty worthy of being shared with all Americans.

Of course, tobacco farming is not limited to our family! Nor is the "Bright Leaf" or "Flue-cured" tobacco we cultivate the only type. Growing any of a dozen different kinds of tobacco is the way of life for hundreds of thousands of farm families throughout the southeastern United States, and has been so since John Rolfe planted those first hills of tobacco at Jamestown in 1612.

This book portrays the tobacco farmer's life, its hardships and its satisfactions. It shows how this life has departed from, yet in many ways carries on the farm methods and values of the past. It also shows the necessity for further change which our technological age is making on tobacco farming—a way of life as old as the country itself.

Pamela Barefoot and Burt Kornegay
August, 1978
Four Oaks, North Carolina

MULES & MEMORIES

"BORN 'N BRED IN MY BONES"

Listen to an oldtimer reminisce about tobacco farming—the good years and the bad, the satisfaction and the worry, the aches and pains from a lifetime of labor—and you can almost imagine him helping John Rolfe set out that very first tobacco crop. His great, great, great, great grandfather may have!

The first European explorers to the New World derived the word tobacco from the Indian "tobago," a Y-shaped wooden tube through which snuff was inhaled. Almost all the North American tribes seem to have grown the plant, which they smoked, chewed, snuffed, and used in tribal ceremonies and for medicinal purposes. Most Europeans, however, found this tobacco very strong and harsh. They preferred the variety growing in the South American colonies of Spain, known as the "Spanish." It was seeds from this tobacco that John Rolfe planted at Jamestown in 1612. Although several previous English settlements had failed in the New World, Jamestown survived in part because tobacco gave it a valuable export commodity to the mother country, where an enjoyment of "fuming" had developed. Throughout the colonial period tobacco remained one of the bases of economic existence. The colonists often used it in place of money—so many pounds of cured leaf, for instance, exchanging for so much flour or gunpowder or rum...or a wife!

As the colonial population multiplied, pioneers moved inland taking tobacco seeds with them. When they settled new areas of the country and planted their seeds tobacco hybrids began to appear. In time many of these came to be preferred to the original Spanish. Burley tobacco, for example, was developed from a hybrid discovered in southern Ohio in the 1860's. When found to be a good chew (the most popular use of tobacco at that time), the cultivation of it spread throughout the hilly and mountainous regions of Kentucky, Tennessee, North Carolina, and Virginia. In a similar way other areas became known for specific kinds of tobacco, and the farmers developed agricultural methods best suited to their particular type.

Today, farmers on the piedmont and coastal plains from Virginia to Florida call Bright Leaf or Flue-cured tobacco—the principal ingredient in cigarettes—their bread and butter crop. Burley, also used in cigarettes, is the primary cash crop for the small farmers of Appalachia. Together these two make up nine-tenths of the acreage grown by the half-a-million tobacco farming families living in the United States. Other tobaccos include the Virgina fire-cured, used in snuff, the chew types grown by the Pennsylvania Dutch, and the cigar-wrapper leaf of Connecticut.

"It's amazing how many tobacco barns you see when
you drive through the Carolinas. There's several sitting
around every house. Looks like everybody there must
be a tobacco farmer."

"We've been raising Burley in our family about as far
back as the family goes."

"When I was five years old, my daddy said to me,
'Get on that tractor, Boy; I've got to set out my 'baccer'.
So I learned how to drive the tractor, and I've been
raising tobacco with him ever since."

"We've kept the country in this farm."

"I reckon we'll farm as long as we're able. We've got
so poor we cain't do nothing *but* farm!"

"We live on hogs and tobacco around here."

"I've done man-work all my life."

"Ain't it a wonder you can put a little-ole seed and some
dirt together and get such a big beautiful plant!"

"I've got a lifetime of learning in tobacco."

"I roll my own cigars. The money not spent on store-bought things my family can spend on groceries."

"Every day I milk three cows and cook for all the help
that works in our tobacco. We have vegetables and a
fresh-baked pie every day. My husband wouldn't think
he was eating if he didn't have a pie."

"I went to college. But I knew when I left what I was going to do. I knew I was coming back here to grow tobacco."

Ila Anderson, Virginia

"I don't remember the first time I saw tobacco. When I woke up in this world they was raising it.

"I cain't even remember what year I was born. I think 1889. I've been afflicted for three or four years and I cain't remember too good. Didn't have much to start with.

"My father, my grandfather, and all were tobacco raisers. My family had to work so hard they were slaves themselves. Let me tell you, tobacco farmers worked!

"When I was a girl, I helped plant tobacco, sucker it, pick off the worms, and everything else. Sometimes they'd get in a hard place and come call me to go help. If I saw them coming, I'd run hide! It was such hard work.

"The menfolks used to cut green wood to make charcoal for curing the tobacco. And they stayed at the barn to watch it cure. Sometimes they fell asleep. One night my husband fell asleep, and when he woke up the top of the barn was roaring in flames! The whole barn burned up. We lost several barns that way.

"They still use those tobacco barns behind my house. My son grows it.

"I used to play with tobacco sticks when I was a little girl. I used them for horses. We had so many tobacco sticks, I reckon I could recognize one a mile away.

"I used to go doodlebug hunting too, yes Lord! 'Doodlebug, doodlebug, come on out; your house is on fire, your house is on fire!' That doodlebug would come out of that hole every time! And do you know, I tried to teach my children that; but they would never learn it; they thought it was so foolish. But when I was a young girl, we'd get off—a big crowd of us girls and boys—and we'd try to see who could make the doodlebug come out first.

"I've never smoked or used snuff. If my momma was living now, and she come back here and found us smoking, she'd whup us to beat all! She wouldn't allow that!

"Farming back then wasn't so bad. Farmers had a good time, yes sir!—on Saturday nights and Sundays."

"Doodlebug, Doodlebug, come on out!"

THE THIRTEEN MONTH CROP

That's how much time tobacco farmers say they need to produce and market their crop—thirteen months!

Long ago tobacco earned its reputation as a plant that required much time and effort to grow. Colonial farmers growled and cussed about the amount of work involved. Today, little has changed in that respect. During the difficulties of the harvest season, farmers carry on something of a contest to see who can most solemnly swear that he'll grow "nary another leaf." However, come fall, they'll be

comparing their acreage for the next year!

Although many types of tobacco are grown in the United States today, almost all tobacco farmers follow one general method in planting and cultivating their crop.

Winter is seedtime. Selecting a site protected from wind, the farmer disks, plows, and harrows the soil for a plant bed. After sterilizing the bed with a gas that rids it of all insect and plant life, he broadcasts the minute seeds over the worked soil, then covers it with a protective canvas or plastic tarp. Under the warmth of the sun the seeds begin to germinate.

In spring the farmer breaks, fertilizes, and ridges the tobacco field itself. When the seedlings have grown about eight inches high, he pulls them from the seedbed by hand and places them in open wooden crates for transplanting to the field. Today most farmers plant the seedlings with a one or two row setter pulled by a tractor. The setter forms the row, drops in the plant, and waters it. Workers riding the machine feed in the seedlings one by one. Some farmers, however, still use horse-drawn setters, and a few continue to transplant by hand.

Throughout spring and early summer the tobacco matures, growing rapidly to five or six feet in height and developing a wrist-sized stalk supporting fifteen to eighteen large, arrowhead-shaped leaves. When the tobacco blossoms, the farmer suckers it and breaks off, or "tops" the white flower-clusters. Removing the blossoms and suckers forces all the plant's nutriments into its main leaves, making them heavier bodied, more aromatic, and better tasting when cured.

In summer the harvest begins. The basic task in harvesting any tobacco is to bring the ripe leaves from the field to the barn where they are cured and, eventually, prepared for market.

Bright Leaf is harvested in several ways. Many farmers still use six to eight "croppers" or "primers" in the field. These workers move down the rows of tall tobacco snapping off the ripened leaves (usually three or four to the stalk) and piling armfuls on wooden trailers. Boys on tractors pull the loaded trailers to the curing barn. Because its leaves ripen in successive stages up the stalk, Bright Leaf must be cropped once a week in this way. The field is completely stripped of leaves, or "tipped" within six to eight weeks.

If the curing barn is the conventional log or plank type, the farmer's wife, daughters, and as many neighbor-women as are needed will be taking the leaves out of the trailers and placing them on the conveyor belt of a "leaf stitcher." This machine sews the leaf butts together so that the leaves straddle a tobacco stick. The leaf-loaded sticks are then hung on wooden tier-poles over an oil or gas burner inside the barn.

A few farmers continue to have the women "loop" or tie the tobacco—bunched in "hands" of three or four leaves—onto the tobacco stick. Most, however, have been forced to abandon this traditional method in the last few years because of a shortage of labor and rising labor costs.

The most mechanized farm operation today uses a bulk barn in conjunction with an automatic harvester in the field. The harvester, operated by one man, strips the leaves to a certain height on the stalk and deposits them in trailers. Workers at the barn pack these leaves into steel racks or large steel boxes and slide them into the barn.

Leaf curing, which takes from five to seven days, is the most delicate aspect of tobacco barning. The farmer must inspect the leaves frequently, raising or lowering the heat inside the barn as they color and dry. When the leaves have "cured-out," they are removed from the barn and wrapped in large burlap sheets. Only then, some nine to ten months after the initial seeding, is the crop ready for market. Hardly has the leaf been sold, however, than the farmer is cutting and uprooting the old stalks in the field and deciding where to plant the next year's crop!

Burley tobacco is harvested just once, in late summer. When the plants have matured, the farmer goes to the field and cuts the stalks at the base. He impales half-a-dozen stalks on a "spear"—a tobacco stick tipped with a metal point—and lets the tobacco stand in the field like this a day or two. When the crop is wilted enough to be handled without breaking, he hauls it to the barn and hangs it on tier poles. Because Burley is cured with natural air, no specially constructed barn is needed. The farmer can use any building on his farm if it has adequate tier space and natural air circulation.

When the Burley is fully cured—a process taking about two months—the farmer removes it from the barn and strips the leaves from the stalks. He grades these leaves and bundles them into "hands." The hands are piled in wooden baskets or placed back on the sticks ready for market.

Whereas the Bright Leaf markets usually open in late July and close in November, the Burley markets don't open until December and remain open through the next March. This means that Burley farmers often sell their leaves *after* they have seeded the next year's plant bed. Theirs truly is a thirteen month crop! ✎

"I reckon the tobacco seed is the smallest seed in the world, smaller than the mustard seed. The Bible says the mustard seed is the smallest, but I believe it's the tobacco seed."

"Thirteen month crop means you have to prepare your new seed bed before you sell your old crop. That happens here."

"The Farmer's Almanac gives you water days and heart days. And you don't plant on heart days, no-sir-ree. Water days is the best."

"I always say, plow in all the fertilizer your pocketbook can stand."

"I set out my Burley with a tin handsetter. I got some
  grandsons to help me set it out. One grandson drops in
  the plant and the other'n gets the water."

"Yesterday I saw one of those setters that the tractor pulls."

"I looked it over good. That's the first time I been up close to one of those."

"The rows that thing set were as straight as an arrow!
Straightest I ever did see!"

"I tell you, there ain't nothing I dread no worse than
to get out in that tobaccer field early in the morning
and get that first wet. That feeling of being good and
wet — boy, that is a bad feeling!"

"Drinktime's the *only* time of day for me!"

"Barning tobacco is like a watch. Everything has got to tick."

"Even now, with the new machinery and stuff, people are busy with tobacco all the time."

"Us Burley farmers still plant by hand, cut by hand,
barn by hand, strip by hand, and tie the leaves into hands.
We're not much ahead of Pocahontas on that."

"It takes about two months to cure our Burley. We just leave the barn door open."

"Here in Lancaster County, we strip the cured leaves and
put them in a wood press. That shapes them into a bale.
The Amish have got such large families, they can get their
children to do it."

"We used to handle each leaf like it was a dollar bill.
Now we walk all over them. If my daddy could see that,
he'd quiver in his grave!"

"It makes you feel about the best you can to know you've got pretty tobacco going to the market!"

Henry and Sadie Williams, Georgia

"To begin with, I was raised on a farm, and all over this county we raised cotton, till the boll weevil put us out of business. So we tried raising peanuts, and everybody bought all the machinery they needed. That done pretty good for a year or two. Then peanuts got to going down, down, down. Didn't bring hardly no money a'tall. Maybe twenty-three dollar to the ton. I remember after a year's hard work I had just two dollar and fifty cent—and no bills paid! So, I stacked up my peanut machinery and decided to try the tobacco business.

"My daddy was one of the first men to plant a hill of tobacco in this part of Georgia. After my daddy planted it, I decided I'd plant me some to see if it'd grow. I got about a dozen hills and set them out beside the fence just to see what they'd do. 'Twas the prettiest crop of tobacco you ever seen!

"Tobacco is the only thing we can depend on for support around here. 'Course, we can get a little extra money out'n a cow or a hog or a soybean, but there ain't much money in corn. If tobacco was to go out, I don't know what folks would do.

"Back then, we sent a mule and a sled out to the field to bring back the tobacco to the barn. There'd be a boy to drive the mule and four men in the field to crop the leaves and put them in the sled. Then we had four stringers at the barn, and four handers, and one to tote the sticks. When they got it all done, two or three croppers would go up in the barn and we'd spend till ten o'clock at night hanging it.

"I used to have a half-dozen mules. I believe I could plow behind a mule all day and not get tired. I'm tough as a mule. We had some good mules in them days. I bet you I couldn't find me two mules in this whole county today.

"I used to say 'Whoa,' 'Gee,' and 'Haw,' to my mules. Whoa means, 'stop,' Gee means, 'a little bit to the right,' and Haw means, 'a little bit to the left.' If I said, 'Git up!' they'd move on ahead. They were right considerate about doing what I told them. They were good, kind mules.

"I wish I had me an old mule."

"Farming is the best life there is. I'd do the same trip
again through life if I could. And I'd marry the same
woman I've been married to for sixty years. I tell
you, we've seen a lot of muddy water pass under the
bridge, but it's been worth it."

"THE MARKET'S NO PLACE FOR A WOMAN"

Is this farmer trying to preserve the masculine atmosphere that for two hundred years has dominated tobacco warehouse auction floors like the aroma of the cured leaf itself? He looks out over the people moving among the long rows of burlap-sheeted tobacco. Yep, not a woman in sight! And if the wives and daughters do come along, they usually stand to one side. He hitches up his suspenders, sure of his domain, and walks over to a group of farmers, joining in the tobacco

talk. The farmers smoke their cigars, look over each other's crop, and swear it's been the dangdest year ever to get that tobacco grown and to the market. They wait for the auctioneer to begin his rapid chant of prices, the chant that will tell them just how much all their work was worth — the most important country music, to their ears, of the year.

Tobacco farmers haven't always sold their crop at public auctions. Colonial farmers, subject to the British tobacco monopoly, grew their leaf for the mother country. They pressure-packed up to one thousand pounds of cured tobacco in hogsheads and rolled or hauled these huge barrels to designated ports for shipment to England. Some farmers, however, especially those far to the south of the major shipping ports in Virginia, sold their crop right off the farm to clever Yankee traders. These traders loaded the tobacco onto small, fast craft, slipped past the British ships, and sailed to New England. There they transferred the tobacco to ocean-going vessels and carried it to wherever they could get the highest price.

After the Revolutionary War, markets around the world opened to American tobacco. Americans themselves began to demand more tobacco products. To sell efficiently the cured leaf being brought to market, warehouse owners began to auction it off to the highest bidder. From this beginning, the present-day auction system evolved.

In the late nineteenth century a "newfangled smoke" called the cigarette began to compete with the old-time favorites: pipe, cigar, snuff, and chew. Burley and Bright Leaf, the principal tobaccos used in cigarettes, became increasingly important. To be closer to the source of these valuable crops, the market system spread from Virginia, where it had been concentrated since the colonial period, to the other tobacco producing states.

Today, there are almost nine hundred auction warehouses operating throughout the Southeast. In these spacious one-story structures covering up to a city block, ninety-five percent of the nation's tobacco crop is sold. The warehouse operators serve as middlemen between the hundreds of thousands of individual farmers and the few tobacco manufacturing companies.

On auction day the farmers truck their sheeted or basketed tobacco to a nearby auction warehouse. Government inspectors weigh and grade the crop, then the warehouseman throws out a bid and sets things going with, "Bid 'er up!" The auctioneer begins to move down the long rows of tobacco chanting prices. Somehow he is able to keep his eye on the dozen or more company buyers who surround him. The buyers signal the prices they are willing to pay by raising a finger, nodding their heads, or even winking. A few have developed the ability to wiggle their ears when the price is right! With such a method a farmer's whole crop, representing up to a year of labor, can be sold in minutes.

...And so the farmers stand beneath the great warehouse ceiling, talking tobacco and waiting for the most important country music of the year to begin. Suddenly four elderly women, carrying a platter piled high with delicious homemade ham biscuits, walk through the warehouse entrance. They're known in the area as the Tart Sisters, and, it turns out, they've been bringing their cured leaf to this warehouse since 1937. They greet the farmers and join in the tobacco talk. If they like the price they get for their crop, they'll pass around the ham biscuits. Even the farmer with the suspenders won't turn one down!

"I've heard some folks say that tobacco warehouse auctions are a schooner ship operation in a jetliner day. But I don't see it that way. Tobacco has got to be sold to human beings, not computers. Someone's got to smell it, feel it, and look at it to buy it."

"As good as I love to run my mouth, it's just my good luck to
get to the market early in the morning and stay all day!"

"I enjoy working as a tobacco auctioneer because I'm
working with people in a situation that's constantly
changing. I enjoy it particularly when the tobacco is
selling well...when you get into a good rhythm and
the buyers sort of waltz along with you."

"There's not as many farmers and people from town
watching the auction as there used to be. I guess people are more
sophisticated now and have other things they'd rather do."

August 2, 1978

"There's a dozen buyers in that line I've got to keep
my eye on. I used to be able to look straight ahead and see
them all at once. Got my eyes to where they'd focus out.
Now I've got to wear these glasses to pull the focus back in."

Life Magazine, November 13, 1939

"People who work public jobs get paid every week. We raise that tobacco and don't get a dime out of it till fall.
Then, time you get all your bills paid and your Christmas money tucked away, you're just about back where you started!"

Roy Pearce, North Carolina

"I began to work in the tobacco market when still a young boy, and I've owned and operated this auction warehouse since 1936.

"I think, without a question, the public auction is the best way to sell tobacco. Most of the farmers who leave here leave satisfied. We've got some farmers who've been selling with us for up to forty years. Some of the old people have passed on, and now their sons and grandsons are selling here.

"When I was a boy on the farm, we'd haul our tobacco to the market with two to four mules or horses hooked to a wagon. We figured on a twelve hour ride. We'd get there, put the animals in the stable under the warehouse, then go upstairs to what was called the camp room. The warehouse would have big pots of coffee there. We'd stand around them and talk and carry on till late at night. Had a great time! In the morning we'd unload the tobacco. 'Course, the farmers don't stay overnight anymore, because they come in trucks.

"We used to have a lot of good dances in this warehouse. At the end of the season we'd get together and invite all our friends, and the whole town would come! We'd have one hundred and fifty couples on the floor dancing!

"I certainly do believe a lot of the enjoyment has gone out of farming. During the barning season, us boys would go around at night from one barn to another trying to catch a man asleep there with his shoes off. We'd put a piece of paper between his toes and set it afire. When it burned down to his toes, he'd jump up with a holler and take out after us! Sometimes we'd go to the creek first and cut his foot-log half in two. Then we'd lead him down to the water. He'd start running across on that foot-log and it'd break and dump him in the creek. He'd come up a-sputtering, but the water would cool off his toes! We had a great time carrying on like that!

"I've seen a lot of good times, a lot of bad times, and a lot of funny times in this warehouse. Most everybody who worked here used to call my wife 'Momma.' They picked it up from me. People would say, 'Momma, where's this?' or 'Momma, where's that?' This old cleaning woman came up to her one day and said, 'Mrs. Pearce, for the good Lord, how many chillen have you got? I ain't never seen so many people come up and say, 'Momma, where's this?' and 'Momma, where's that?'"

MULES AND MEMORIES

Bulk barns, automatic harvesters, leaf stitchers? These are integral to tobacco farming today. But just thirty years ago most farmers would have thought they were words from a foreign language! Mules, plows, pegs, and sweat were what they knew: direct, one-syllable words. If you had asked to see their machinery, chances are they would have held forth two hands.

Tobacco is still America's largest cash crop that is most dependent on the human hand. Almost three hundred hours of labor must be put into the cultivation and marketing of every acre. In comparison, it now takes no more than four hours to farm an acre of wheat! Of all tobaccos, Bright Leaf has been most receptive to mechanization. Yet as late as 1960 the farming of it had changed little since the previous century. Even today the suckering, topping, cropping, and hanging of that crop remain a vital work heritage.

Thirty years ago, however, no one would have thought of calling any aspect of tobacco farming a "work heritage." It was all just work! And there was enough of it for everyone to have as much as they wanted, and then some.

Maybe that's why tobacco farmers liked their mules. Maybe that's the reason they talk about old Doll and Della or Mag and Kate with such a fond tone. Of course, when they actually owned Doll or Della, the farmers probably didn't have much more to say about them than a couple of brief, earthy epithets that are best not mentioned. However, even then they knew that those long-eared, sure-footed, eleven hundred ornery pounds of pull-power could turn the ground with a plow like no earthly man!

It was not uncommon for a mule to live twenty-five years. That mule would become like a member of the farmer's family. The farmer had to feed his mule in the morning before he ate breakfast himself, and feed it again at night before he took off his boots and stretched his aching toes to the fire. When the mule got sick there was doctoring to do. When either the mule or the farmer woke up in a bad mood, a fight was sure to follow before bedtime came around. And, whether he liked it or not, that mule's hind end was the farmer's primary scenery for a considerable portion of each day!

When the tractor came along in the late 1940's, it seemed like the world had suddenly changed—many farmers felt for the worse. But they had to admit that a man and a mule could plow no more than two acres of ground in a day, while a man with a tractor could plow three or four acres every hour! That was the difference. And to farmers with families to feed and hopes for some material better-ment in life, the choice was obviously for the mule on wheels.

Oldtimers rarely look back on any aspect of their pre-tractor farming years without emotion. Many tend to see the bright side of that life. They recall such rural pleasures as skinny-dipping in a ''black water'' creek and warehouse dances at the end of the market season which have now all but disappeared from the land. Others shake their heads, tighten their jaws, and talk in hard, uncompromising terms. They remember the thirst and sweat of the field, the day after day necessity to labor as if life itself depended on it—which, in many cases, it did.

The truth about the past includes both of these memories and all that lie between the two extremes. Maybe for some, life was more en-joyable or more difficult than for others. With many farmers it is not only their words, but the weathering of their faces, which expresses for the nation a largely untold and almost forgotten story. ◁

"Used to be we didn't know what an hour's wage was.
We'd go out a little after light and work till just
before dark, and be glad to get our twenty-five cent."

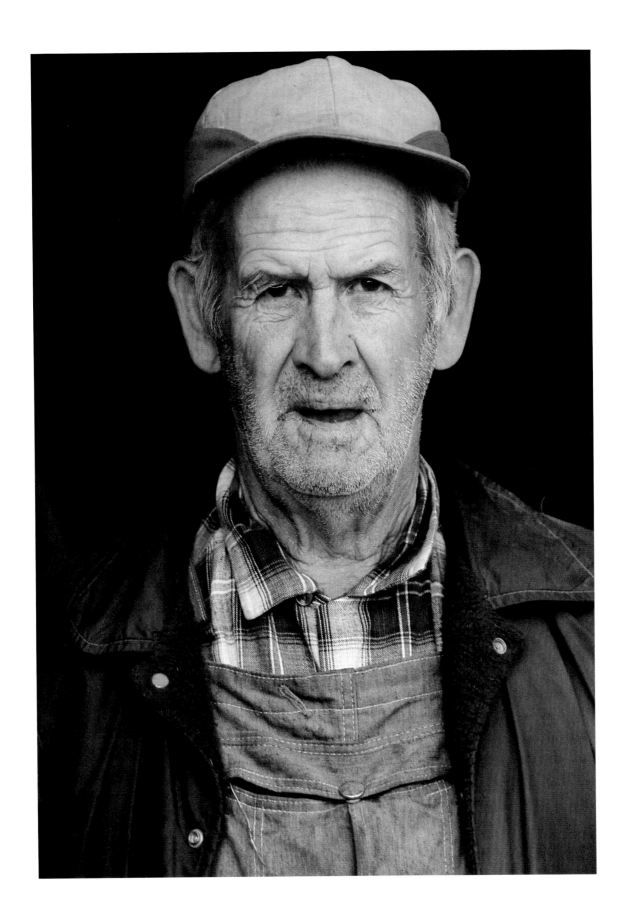

"I remember the first car around. Old Lady Johnson
had it. We'd walk way out yonder to the road every Sunday
just to see it pass. I reckon kids today would walk out
there to see a horse and wagon."

"I used to put spark plugs on my tobacco stick so that when
I rode it, it'd be the fastest horse around!"

"You know, I hadn't ever thought about this before, but every once in a while you had to have a fight with your mule. Yes, you had to have a fight with your mule."

"A mule will do a lot of things to irk you. But maybe
when you shouldn't be. Maybe it's not always the mule
much worse than it is the man."

"I got my first tractor in 1945. A lot of folks said,
'I wouldn't have that thing in my field, I'd run it out. It'll
pack the dirt'. Then people got to doing such pretty
work with their tractors everybody had to have one.
After a while there won't no more mules around."

"On the farm it just don't seem right not to have a mule.
I like a mule to look at for what it has been."

"When labor was cheap, we used to pick off tobacco
worms and throw them on the ground and stomp on them.
But I think that was more to the satisfaction of the farmer
than it was an actual gain."

"I call my son 'my little boy', even though he's sixty-eight years old. But you know I made a girl out of him this summer! Had him help me can and fix the vegetables. I think I'll make a cook out of him instead of a farmer."

"Barning tobacco isn't like it used to be. It's more work,
work, work. We used to get a crowd together and have
tobacco tyings. We'd all be telling jokes and laughing
and having a good time!"

"I still use a horse to cultivate my tobacco. I talk to
her and she knows just what to do. You cain't talk to
a tractor like that. Somebody'd look at you funny."

"Most people used to get up before the rooster and be
ready to go plowing at first light, and walk along behind that
mule all day. You couldn't be in too big a hurry, 'cause you
was both walking. Now, that was modern farming back then."

Lillie Tart, North Carolina

"My mother, Lucy, and me and my sisters, Addie, Bessie, and Lessie, started tending tobacco in 1937. We did all the work. Sometimes we'd swap with the neighbors, maybe work on ourn one day and theirn the next.

"We plowed tobacco, corn, and cotton with mules. We had two mules, Mag and Kate. One was black and the other was kinda brown. They were smart mules, until we got so old and feeble we couldn't do nothing with them, and then they'd run away!

"I had the mule run away with me up yonder across the road one time. Hooked to the plow, I mean! I was up there plowing and that mule broke away and run and went toward the house, and Bessie happened to see her a-coming. She went right to the door and met her and said, 'WHOA!' And that mule stopped just as sudden as you've ever seen. You know, that unnerved me so bad. I was running along behind that mule, but you know I couldn't catch up with her. A mule is fast! And that plow just a-flying around her head! It's a wonder it didn't get cut off! I don't believe there's any mules left in this part of the country now.

"Back then, an acre of tobacco was something to set out. There won't setting machines and all. When we transplanted the little plants, we used a long peg. We'd stick it in the ground and make a hole and put the plant in and water it and then fill up the hole.

"Then, when it growed and bloomed out, we had to top and sucker it. I remember getting just as wet as a dog a-suckering. You had to pull them suckers out or your tobacco wouldn't make nothing. Lots of time we'd have to barn tobacco every day of the week and then get out there and sucker it. Sometimes it would be so hot you couldn't hardly stay out there.

"People used to get the mumps, and sometimes it'd go down on the men and they'd near 'bout die. They'd take a plug of tobacco and keep it bound to them down there, and they'd get better.

"I still help tend tobacco when I'm able. I help get the cured tobacco ready for market. You know, I love to go to the market!"

"You know, if a wasp or anything stings you, you rub it good
with wet snuff and it will ease the pain off."

"I LIKES MY OWN IDEAS"

Tobacco farmers don't need to hang signs over their fireplaces reminding them that home is sweet. They know it is! The land they live on produces for them; they understand it. Their friends are like kin and their kin are like friends; they understand each other. They know what can be asked of both land and friends, and what will be asked in return. As a group they probably travel or move as little as

any Americans. There are few other places they want to be. Their hearts and minds, along with the crops, are rooted in the soil they till.

In spite of this domestic nature, however, tobacco farmers are also gamblers. Hail, flood, drought, disease, and fire threaten the crops from seedtime through the harvest. And farmers know these natural forces can not only threaten—but strike. More than a few families have lost their curing barn to fire. If a stick of dried leaves falls out of the tiers onto a burner, the barn ignites like an oil-soaked torch. The rest of the year's crop will just about cover the loss. Even if it is a successful year and a high-grade leaf goes to market, the price it will bring from the buyers can never be foretold.

Yet each spring the farmers set out the plants, because, notwithstanding the uncertainty of their way of life, they are believers. They believe that although disasters come, blessings come as well. They believe in hard work and its eventual reward. They have faith that a power greater than their own or nature's will see them through the year.

At times, however, it must seem as if they're having to wait "a right good spell" for that help to get there! And it's from the waiting that they've learned how to laugh—at themselves, at others, and at the whole unpredictable business called farming. During the most calamitous of days someone will tell a joke. It's also during hardship that tobacco farmers rely more than ever on know-how gained from experience. The classroom is the field. Book knowledge has its place, but back-and-shoulder knowledge is essential to make the most of each year.

Above all, tobacco farmers value the independence and self-sufficiency of the small-farming life. They may never have heard of Thomas Jefferson's desire to make this a nation of sturdy, stable, and hard-working agrarian citizens, but perhaps that's because they've been too busy in the fields! Tobacco farmers are one of the largest remaining groups of agrarian citizens in the United States.

Some oldtimers declare that today "all the work's been worked-out of farming." In some ways, they're right. The cords of wood once used for flue-curing in summer took the whole winter to cut by hand. Today the farmer simply flicks an oil burner's switch. Farm life in general is less strenuous. A faucet, rather than a pot on the stove, now brings hot water into the house.

Yet in many ways farming still requires as much work as ever. The hours of hand labor necessary to farm tobacco have been halved in the last thirty years, but today's farmer is likely to be growing twice as much tobacco as his father or grandfather. And for the croppers and cutters, it's hot as ever in the fields. Moreover, the purchase of expensive machinery and the finding of reliable help with the harvest are problems that were never known by the farmers of yesterday.

Some oldtimers lament that all the fun's gone out of farming. Once again, they're right. The age demands speed, efficiency, and uniformity of method. Farmers find themselves increasingly tied up with the mechanics of agriculture as a thing apart from the integrated community life that has always been one of the rewards of a rural existence. Many feel they're always on the run. Family ties seem stretched. "Down home" fun to the young often seems cornpone.

However, anyone who sits with the farmers at the country store in the evening or works with them in the fields, knows the deep satisfaction and pervasive sense of humor that enrich their lives. Families still work and celebrate together. Pig-pickings and barbecues mark the last day of the harvest season. A farmer is likely to end his day's work with a fishing pole down at the pond.

As for fun, well, once a year Uncle So-and-so bogs down his tractor in the field, then gets several more stuck trying to pull out the first, and everyone within hearing distance can sit back and chuckle while he cusses those tractors all the way to firmer ground!

A new kind of tobacco farming *is* emerging. The farmers themselves are most aware of it. The silver gleam of bulk barns and the clank of machinery become more noticeable each year. Yet many of the most obvious "changes" are deceptive. Beneath the surface, the heart of farming is much the same, the problems to overcome the same. Thirty years ago the mule might get sick the night before harvest; today the tractor may break down.

What does the future hold for the American tobacco farmer? Can he assimilate the agricultural technology of our age in a small-farming way? One thing is certain: though adapt he must, the values and farm methods he has inherited from the past, as well as the sensitive nature of the tobacco plant itself, will influence and temper that change. ❧

"I've said a lot of times that as much as the Lord's been good to us all, people's been mighty good to me."

"That northern machinery is changing the scene around here."

"I lost my wife two months ago. We'd been married fifty-
three years, and I loved her as good the last day as I did the
first.'Course, I love most everybody. But she was the
only one ever made me feel the love that says, 'I do.'"

"If they took my tobacco away from me, *worry'd* cause me to get cancer!"

"Looks to me like the small farmer is about to get out of whack."

"It gets rough. It'll drain you down. But, to me, the harder it is, the better I like it."

"Lord, I've worked in tobacco all my life. Don't know that I didn't even sleep in it. Probably be buried in it too."

"You know how to tell a level-headed farmer when you see one? He's got tobacco juice running out both sides of his mouth at the same time!"

"Back then to be a good farmer you had to have get-up-and-go.
Nowadays to be a good farmer you've got to have machinery."

"You couldn't pay us to live in no city. If we lived in
the city, we'd sure have to fight!"

"Drove clear down to Miami once, me and my wife. Took two days! Drove to where there was a sign saying, DEAD END, DEEP WATER. I got out and looked around, thought to myself, 'I wouldn't give ten cents for this'. So we got in the truck and come on back."

"I lost my tobacco to hail one time. It beat it all down.
We had just set it out, and the hail came. We just turned
around and set it all out again."

Con Johnson, Virginia

"I'm passed eighty years old and still trying to pull a hundred. I still work in tobaccer a little, but I cain't get nothing out'n it, 'cept tired.

"I got a little good land. But most of it ain't no 'count. You got to buy a lot of sorry mountain land to get a few acres of good land or a good holler for planting 'baccer. I hear-tell that land in Virginny where George Washington plowed is pretty land.

"I got a barn over yonder and a couple more barns down in the holler where I hang my 'baccer to cure-out. Got a few more over there on Copper Crick.

"I hate to talk about tobaccer in the Hoover Days. Me and my daddy growed an acre of Burley and carried it over to the market, and it brought just fifteen dollars. We swore we'd never raise another leaf, and *he* never did! But I broke over and growed it, and everybody said I swore a lie.

"Way back then, raising tobaccer was hard work. The more you work the older you get. Now, a pretty woman shouldn't have to work nary a lick!

"I used to chaw homemade. That's what I call the poor man's 'baccer.

"I'm gonna try to get me some tobaccer growed this year. But I cain't get no help. 'Course, my grandson, Lyndon Baines, and another one I call Harry Truman will help me out. If they don't work any more than they do now, they'll do pretty good!"

"I like to watch my tobacco grow. I go out there every morning and look at it, make sure it's all right, tend to it, and study things about it. I like it. I sure do."

AIR-CURED: Tobacco cured by the circulation of natural air, a process which takes about two months. Nearly all cigar tobaccos, as well as Burley "light" and "dark" types, are air-cured.

AUTOMATIC HARVESTER: Recently developed harvesting machine, usually operated by one man, which strips Flue-cured tobacco leaves from the stalk so they may be prepared for curing.

BALE: A fifty to sixty pound case of cured tobacco leaves ready to be sold to tobacco companies. Pennsylvania tobacco is baled.

BARNING: The process of harvesting and curing tobacco. Also referred to as "housing" in some areas.

BASKET: A shallow basket made of woven wooden strips which holds cured tobacco ready for the market.

BRIGHT LEAF: Gas or oil heat-cured tobacco, grown on the piedmont and coastal plains from Virginia to Florida and used primarily in cigarettes. Also called "Flue-cured."

BULK BARN: Recently developed barn which cures Bright Leaf tobacco with forced hot air.

BURLEY: Type of air-cured tobacco grown mainly in Kentucky and Tennessee and used primarily in cigarettes.

CASE: The condition cured tobacco leaves are said to be in after they have reabsorbed the moisture content in natural air following the curing process. Cured tobacco is not limber enough to be prepared for market until allowed to come "in case." This process is also called "ordering."

CONVENTIONAL BARN: Specially constructed barn in which Bright Leaf tobacco is cured with oil or gas heat, a process which takes five to seven days.

CROPPER: Field worker who harvests, primes, or pulls off the ripe Bright Leaf tobacco leaves from the stalk.

CULTIVATE: To work the soil between the plants with mule or tractor-drawn equipment.

CURING: The process of drying the sap in freshly harvested tobacco either by exposure to heat or natural air.

CUTTER: Field worker who harvests mature Burley tobacco by cutting the entire stalk close to the ground and impaling this stalk on a "spear."

FLUE-CURED: Also called "Bright Leaf." The bright yellow color of the cured leaf is due mainly to the character of the soil in which it is grown and the method of curing.

HAND: A bundle of cured, graded leaves tied at the butt with a tobacco leaf of a similar grade.

HANDER: Barn worker who passes cropped tobacco leaves in bunches of three or four from the trailer to the "looper" or "stringer" who ties the leaves to a tobacco stick with twine.

HANDSETTER: Long, narrow tube made of aluminum or tin which is used in transplanting the tobacco seedlings in spring.

HILL: A plant rooted with a small mound of soil heaped around the roots.

HORNWORM: Large, bright green worm which eats the tobacco leaves from the stalk. Usually called the tobacco worm.

LOOPER: Barn worker who ties the cropped leaves to tobacco sticks in preparation for curing.

MULE: Domestic animal that is the offspring of a male jackass and a female horse. Characterized by long ears and short mane and well-known for endurance.

PACKHOUSE: Barn or shelter where flue-cured tobacco is stored, graded, and sheeted for market.

PEG: A wooden stick with which tobacco seedlings were set out in the field before the invention of the handsetter and the automatic setter.

PLANT BED: Loamy soil specially prepared in winter for sowing tobacco seeds.

PRIMING: In Flue-cured areas, the harvest of leaves as they mature.

SETTER: Tractor-drawn machine which transplants tobacco seedlings in the field.

SHEET: Large burlap tarp in which cured Bright Leaf tobacco is wrapped prior to taking it to market.

SPEAR: Tobacco stick tipped with a sharp metal point on which cut air-cured tobacco stalks are impaled and hung in the barn to cure.

STRIPPING: The removal of the air-cured leaf from the stalk and the Flue-cured leaf from the tobacco stick so the cured leaves may be prepared for market.

SUCKERS: Secondary growths of leaves which sprout between the main tobacco leaves and the stalk.

TIER: A row or layer of tobacco after it has been hung in the curing barn.

TOPPING: Removing the blossoms and sometimes the top leaves from the tobacco plant to encourage the growth of its main leaves.

TRUCKING: To bring the cropped leaves from the field to the barn in a tractor-drawn trailer or a mule-drawn sled.